Quick Guide to FINANCIAL LITERACY

Carla Mooney

ReferencePoint Press

San Diego, CA

ReferencePoint Press®

Printed in the United States

For more information, contact:
ReferencePoint Press, Inc.
PO Box 27779
San Diego, CA 92198
www.ReferencePointPress.com

LIBRARY OF CONGRESS CATALOGING-IN-PUBLICATION DATA

Name: Mooney, Carla- author
Title: Quick Guide to Financial Literacy/by Carla Mooney
Description: San Diego, CA: ReferencePoint Press, Inc, 2027.
| Includes bibliographical references and index.
Identifiers: LCCN 2026019770 (print) | ISBN
9781678213503 library binding | ISBN 9781678213510 ebook
Subjects: LCSH: Juvenile literature

For compete cataloging-in-publication data please go to www.loc.gov.

CONTENTS

The Basics of Financial Health

Getting into financial trouble can cost a lot of time and money, as many adults know all too well. Learning the basics about money and finances can prevent future issues. In January 2026, 180 middle school and high school students took early steps toward financial literacy at the Financial Literacy Retreat and Reality Fair. The event, held at Nash Community College, was sponsored by Communities In Schools of North Carolina, a nonprofit organization that works with schools to help students succeed. The students learned important financial skills and participated in activities and discussions on how to manage money wisely so they could avoid financial pitfalls in the future.

At the event, students learned basic financial skills, such as creating a budget and shopping for insurance. They learned how to manage childcare costs and other real-life expenses. Students participated in a real-life simulation in which they were given a job, salary, expenses to plan for, and the occasional unexpected bill, such as a car repair or medical bill. They moved from station to station in the simulation and practiced using the financial skills they had learned. Community volunteers from local businesses, banks, and industries helped guide students through each step of the program.

Afterward, students talked about what they learned at the event. Kemora Battle, a senior at Rocky Mount High School, initially believed many adults struggled financially because they did not earn enough money. She was surprised to learn at the fair that the bigger problem is that many adults do not know how

> **"If you learn how to be financially literate, you are already ahead of many others. I believe financial literacy is a key factor in building a successful future."[3]**
>
> —Nathan Cooper, high school senior

to manage their money. "I was surprised by how important budgeting, saving, and understanding credit are in everyday life,"[1] she says. Eighth-grader Kemarus Mercer learned the value of saving his earnings and the importance of budgeting for expenses. "I learned that I need to keep my money safe,"[2] he says.

Nathan Cooper, another senior at Rocky Mount High School, said that the event helped him realize the importance of financial literacy for his future. "If you learn how to be financially literate, you are already ahead of many others. I believe financial literacy is a key factor in building a successful future,"[3] he says.

Being Smart with Money

Money decisions affect everyday life. Each day, people make choices about how they use their money, such as buying groceries, paying for transportation, or deciding whether to save or spend extra cash. Small decisions can add up over time. For example, regularly

Money decisions affect everyday life. Each day, people make choices about how they use their money, such as buying groceries or deciding whether to save or spend extra cash.

spending money on unnecessary items may make it harder to save for something important, like a car, college, or a home.

Yet despite the importance of financial decisions, many Americans struggle to understand basic money management. Less than 50 percent of Americans understood basic financial principles in 2024, according to the World Economic Forum. As a result, nearly half of American adults may struggle to make informed financial decisions. American adults are also struggling to save adequately for both short-term and long-term goals. More than one-third of American adults have more credit card debt than money saved for emergencies, according to a 2023 report from financial information providers Annuity.org and Bankrate. In addition, the same report found that 68 percent of American adults would not be able to cover one month of living expenses if they lost their main source of income.

Having strong financial literacy skills can help people make informed decisions about their money and finances. Financial literacy means understanding how money works and making smart decisions about it. It includes learning how to earn money, spend it wisely, save for the future, and avoid unnecessary debt. Being financially literate helps people manage their money responsibly and plan for both short-term needs and long-term goals. Without these skills, they may struggle to pay bills, build savings, or prepare for unexpected expenses. Learning about money early helps people feel more confident and in control of their financial future.

Henry Leverett worked as a financial literacy program manager at Queensborough National Bank & Trust Company in Georgia. After seeing the importance of financial literacy in his own life, he was inspired to help others improve their own financial skills. "I've seen hardworking, honest people struggle because they didn't have a proper financial education. I want to see this change—through sound financial advice and education, early in life, for everyone,"[4] he says.

CHAPTER ONE

Money and Income

Money plays a major role in everyday life. People use money to buy food, pay for housing, travel, and save for the future. Yet many people use money every day without fully understanding how it works. Financial literacy begins with learning the basics of money, including where it comes from, how people earn it, and how they spend it.

Money: A Medium of Exchange

Long ago, people traded to get the goods and services they needed. This system of trading is known as bartering. For example, a farmer might trade eggs for bread from a baker. A doctor might treat a rancher's family in exchange for a cow. While bartering worked in small communities, it became difficult when people needed many different items or could not agree on equal value. Money solved this problem by providing a standard way to measure value. Instead of trading goods and services directly, people could sell items for money and then use that money to buy other needed items or services.

Money can be easily exchanged, measured, and saved. Money is a medium of exchange, which means people use it to buy and sell goods and services. For example, a shirt might cost twenty dollars, whereas a pair of shoes might cost sixty dollars. Unlike bartering goods such as eggs or milk, which must be used before they spoil, money can be easily saved and used later.

Currency is the official money used in a country. In the United States, the main currency is the US dollar. Different countries use different currencies. For example, Europe uses the euro,

Japan uses the yen, and the United Kingdom uses the pound. When people travel or trade internationally, they often need to exchange one currency for another.

Coins, Bills, and Digital Money

For many years, currency primarily consisted of coins and paper bills. In recent years, however, fewer people are using physical paper money and coins. Instead, more people are turning to digital money.

Digital money exists only in electronic form and is used for online or electronic transactions. Instead of being printed like paper bills or minted like coins, digital money is stored on computers, phones, or banking systems. People can use it to buy goods and services, pay bills, or send money to others through apps, debit cards, credit cards, or online banking.

For example, when someone pays for a purchase with a debit card or sends money through a payment app such as Zelle or PayPal, the money moves digitally between bank accounts instead of being handed over as physical cash. Many businesses and people use digital money every day because it is fast and convenient. Banks and financial institutions keep records of these digital transactions, allowing people to send and receive money quickly without handling physical cash.

Cryptocurrency

In recent years, a new form of digital money, cryptocurrency, has grown in popularity. Cryptocurrency is a type of digital money that people can use to make online payments or store value online. However, cryptocurrency differs from other digital money in a few ways. A government or central bank controls most digital money. Therefore, digital payments still use currency, such as the US dollar or euro, which are created by governments and managed by central banks. When people pay with a digital payment app, such as Venmo, they transfer US dollars or another government-issued currency.

Money can be easily exchanged, measured, and saved. Money is a medium of exchange, which means people use it to buy and sell goods and services.

In contrast, cryptocurrencies are not controlled by governments or central banks. Instead, cryptocurrencies use computer programs and special codes to record transactions and control the total supply of cryptocurrency. Owners store cryptocurrency in digital wallets and can use it to buy goods and services or to send money to other people over the internet. When someone sends cryptocurrency, a public digital ledger called a blockchain records the transaction, helping prevent fraud and tracking ownership.

Government currencies have value because they are recognized as legal money by the country. In the past, the value of some currencies was also tied to valuable resources, such as gold or silver. In comparison, a cryptocurrency's value mostly depends on technology, supply, and demand. Some cryptocurrencies are designed so that only a limited amount of each can ever be created. Because of this scarcity, the price can rise if many people want to buy it. Its value can change based on how much people trust the technology and how much interest investors have in it.

One of the most well-known cryptocurrencies is Bitcoin, which was created in 2009. Since then, thousands of other

The value of digital cryptocurrencies, like Bitcoin, can change quickly. Therefore, financial experts recommend that people learn all about cryptocurrency before using it.

cryptocurrencies have been developed. People like cryptocurrency because transactions can be fast and global, and it does not require a traditional bank. However, cryptocurrency can be risky. The value of cryptocurrencies can change quickly, making them more volatile than traditional money. Therefore, financial experts recommend that people learn carefully about cryptocurrency before using it.

Earning Money

One of the most important parts of financial literacy is understanding how people earn money. The money a person earns is called income. Income can usually be classified into one of three categories: earned, passive, or investment.

Most people earn income through work, usually by having a job where they perform tasks or provide services in exchange for payment. However, workers can be paid in several different ways. Some workers earn wages for each hour they work, whereas others earn a fixed annual salary. Some workers, especially those in sales jobs, earn commissions, which are payments based on how

“The gig economy has earned a strong reputation among workers as a reliable source of income that allows for unparalleled flexibility.”[5]

—Tracey Lazos, senior director of TransUnion’s gig economy business

much they sell. Workers in service jobs, such as restaurant servers or hairstylists, may earn tips from customers. Some people earn income through a business they own that sells goods or provides services.

In the modern gig economy, some people earn income through independent freelance work. For example, they might freelance as a writer, babysitter, or rideshare driver to earn income. In 2024, 62 percent of US adults earned income from one or more gig jobs, according to research by credit reporting agency TransUnion. For 37 percent of adults, gig work was their primary source of income. “The gig economy has earned a strong reputation among workers as a reliable source of income that allows for unparalleled flexibility,” says Tracey Lazos, the senior director of TransUnion’s gig economy business. “Our research indicates that this trend is likely to continue as more seek a primary or supplementary income from gig work.”[5]

Unlike earned income, passive income is money that a person receives without actively working for it on a daily basis. Often, passive income requires an up-front investment of time or money. For example, people who own rental properties and collect rent payments from tenants earn passive income. However, they incurred up-front costs to buy the property and must pay ongoing

Employee vs. Independent Contractor

When working for a company, some people are employees and others are hired as independent contractors. They often perform the same tasks, but there are some important differences. An employee works directly for a company or organization. The employer controls the schedule, tasks, and work environment. Employees usually receive regular paychecks and have taxes automatically deducted from their earnings.

Independent contractors, on the other hand, work for themselves and provide services to different clients. Independent contractors have more freedom in choosing their work, but they also have more responsibility. They must keep track of their income, pay their own taxes, and often provide their own health insurance or retirement savings. Examples of independent contractors include freelance writers, graphic designers, rideshare drivers, and consultants.

maintenance costs to keep it in good shape. "Many people think that passive income is about getting something for nothing," says Todd Tresidder, a financial coach. "It has a 'get-rich-quick' appeal . . . but in the end, it still involves work. You just give the work upfront."[6] Other examples of passive income include royalties from creative works and sponsored social media posts.

Natalie Moore owns a beach house in Ocean Grove, New Jersey, and earns passive income by renting it to guests. Moore and her husband manage the property themselves, book guest stays, and perform routine maintenance. "You have to always keep the renter in mind," she says. "Keep your house accessible, keep your house up—you want to make sure you don't get a bad review."[7]

> **"Many people think that passive income is about getting something for nothing. It has a 'get-rich-quick' appeal . . . but in the end, it still involves work. You just give the work upfront."[6]**
>
> —Todd Tresidder, financial coach

Investment income is money earned from a person's stocks, bonds, and other investments. It includes interest from savings, money market, and certificate of deposit accounts. Investment income also includes money made from selling stocks or other investments that have increased in value. Stock dividends—when a company pays shareholders part of its earnings—are also a form of investment income. Understanding where income comes from is important because it affects how people budget, save, and plan for the future. For example, income from a job is often more regular and predictable than investment income, making it easier to rely on for budgets and savings plans.

Employment Basics

For most people, working is the primary way they earn income—performing job tasks in exchange for pay. Some jobs are full-time, and employees work about forty hours per week. In addition to pay, full-time workers may also receive benefits such as health insurance, retirement plans, and paid vacation or sick time.

Other jobs are part-time. Employees work fewer hours and may not receive benefits. Many teens and young adults start earning

Many teens and young adults start earning income through part-time jobs such as working as a cashier at a retail store, a server at a restaurant, or a lifeguard at a community pool.

income through part-time jobs such as working as a cashier at a retail store, a server at a restaurant, or a lifeguard at a community pool.

Understanding a Paycheck

When employees are paid, they receive a paycheck or a digital pay stub. This document shows how much money they earned and how much was deducted for taxes and other expenses. Gross pay is the amount employees earn before deductions. However, gross pay is not the amount they receive in their bank account. Instead, taxes and deductions are taken out first.

Common tax deductions include federal income tax, state income tax, social security tax, and Medicare tax. Some employees may also have city or local taxes deducted from their pay. Other deductions include health insurance premiums, retirement account contributions, or union fees. After all deductions are taken out, the amount the worker actually receives is called net pay or take-home pay.

Seventeen-year-old Tommy Richmond was excited to get his first paycheck from his new job. He estimated his pay based on the number of hours he had worked over the past two weeks. However, when he opened his pay stub, he was stunned. The check amount was less than what he had expected. "At first I was kind of confused as to why there was any money coming out of my paycheck at all,"[8] he says. Richmond talked to his mother, Traci Richmond, a financial adviser, who explained that he had forgotten to factor in tax withholdings and deductions. Richmond quickly learned how to read his pay stub and to understand the difference between gross pay and net pay.

Income Tax Basics

Taxes are payments that individuals and businesses make to the government. When an employee receives a paycheck, taxes are usually withheld, meaning the employer sends part of the employee's earnings directly to the government. Withholding taxes from each paycheck helps the employee avoid a large tax bill at the end of the year.

Governments use tax money to fund public services such as schools, roads, emergency services, and national defense. Income tax is one of the most common types of taxes. It is based on a person's earnings. In the United States, the income tax system is

What Is Net Worth?

Net worth is a measure of a person's financial health. It shows how much wealth someone has by comparing what they own (assets) to what they owe (liabilities). This is the formula to calculate net worth: assets – liabilities = net worth.

Assets are things a person owns that have value. Assets can include money in a savings account, investments such as stocks or bonds, retirement accounts, property, vehicles, jewelry, and other valuable items. Liabilities are debts or financial obligations, such as credit card balances, student loans, car loans, medical bills, or a home mortgage.

Net worth is the difference between a person's assets and liabilities. When assets are greater than debts, net worth is positive. When debts are higher than assets, net worth is negative. Understanding net worth helps people measure their financial health and plan for the future.

progressive, so people who earn more usually pay a higher percentage of their income in taxes.

> "Developing personal finance skills is as important as learning how to read and write."[9]
>
> —Annamaria Lusardi, senior fellow at the Stanford Institute for Economic Policy Research

Filing a Tax Return

Each year, most workers must file tax returns with the federal and state governments. A tax return is a form that reports how much money people earned and how much tax they paid during the year. The government uses tax returns to determine whether people paid the correct amount of taxes. Tax returns are due by April 15 unless a person files a special form requesting an extension.

People file their federal tax returns with the Internal Revenue Service (IRS) and their state tax returns with the appropriate state agency. Many people use tax software to complete their tax returns. Some hire tax professionals to help prepare their returns.

Sometimes, people qualify for tax deductions. A deduction reduces the amount of income subject to tax. As a result, deductions can reduce the total tax a person owes. Common deductions include contributions to retirement accounts, mortgage interest payments, charitable donations, and certain education expenses.

Sometimes people pay too much in taxes during the year through paycheck withholding. When this happens, they may receive a tax refund. Other times, people may not have paid enough taxes and must send additional money to the government with their tax returns.

Why Understanding Money Matters

Learning about money and income is the first step toward becoming financially responsible. When you understand the basics of money, you are better prepared to create a budget, save for future goals, and avoid unnecessary debt. "Developing personal finance skills is as important as learning how to read and write,"[9] says Annamaria Lusardi, a senior fellow at the Stanford Institute for Economic Policy Research. The decisions you make about money today can shape your financial future for many years to come.

CHAPTER TWO

Budgeting and Smart Spending

Once you earn or receive money, whether from a job, an allowance, gifts, or a small business, it becomes important to learn to manage it carefully. Many people think that money problems crop up only when someone does not earn enough. In reality, money problems often occur because people spend more than they earn or do not follow a budget.

> "[Budgeting] gives you control over your money, allowing you to make informed decisions about spending, saving, and investing."[10]
>
> —Taylor Kovar, certified financial planner

Budgeting helps you control your spending and plan for the future. Making a budget is like creating a road map for your money and financial future. "It gives you control over your money, allowing you to make informed decisions about spending, saving, and investing,"[10] says Taylor Kovar, a certified financial planner.

Budgeting Basics

A budget is a plan for how money will be used. It shows how much money is coming in (income) and how much is being spent (expenses) or saved. This helps you decide how much to spend or set aside for future goals. You can make a budget for a month, several months, or a whole year.

Creating a budget offers more control over where money goes, rather than wondering where it went at the end of the month. "This control is crucial for avoiding overspending and for ensuring that your financial resources are being used effectively to meet your goals,"[11] Kovar says.

Teen Dallin Gariety relies on a budget to help him manage his money. "My parents have a rule: they will pay for half of whatever extra thing I want, and I have to pay for the other half," he says. "For example, if I want to drive a car, I need to come up with the money to pay for half of the insurance and half of the gas. If I want to go on a trip with a school group, I need to come up with the money to pay for half of the fees associated with it. To make sure I have enough money for these extra things, I created budgets."[12]

Tracking Income and Expenses

The first step in making a budget is to track income and expenses. Income is any money received. For many people, income comes from a job or a regular paycheck. Teens might earn income from part-time work, babysitting, mowing lawns, or other work. Some people may also receive money from allowances, gifts, freelance work, or side jobs. Recording all sources of income shows the total amount of money available to spend or save.

Expenses are money paid for goods or services. Some expenses are fixed, which means they usually stay the same each month. For example, rent, car payments, and phone bills are often

A budget is a plan for how a person will use their money. It shows how much money is coming in and how much is being spent or saved.

fixed expenses a person pays each month. Other expenses are variable and change from month to month. Groceries, entertainment, clothing, and eating out are examples of variable expenses. Tracking both types reveals where you spend money.

There are several ways to track income and expenses. Some people write them down in a notebook. Others enter them into a spreadsheet or use a budgeting app such as Goodbudget or EveryDollar. Each time you earn or spend money, you should record it. Over time, a detailed picture emerges of your income and spending patterns.

Tracking expenses often reveals surprises. Small purchases, such as a four-dollar coffee, might seem insignificant. Over time, however, these small purchases can add up and become a much larger part of monthly spending. For example, you might discover that buying a four-dollar coffee most mornings adds up to eighty dollars in a month. Seeing these patterns and how they add up can make it easier to decide whether that is where you want to spend your money.

Tracking income and expenses also allows you to compare how much money is coming in and going out. If expenses exceed

Setting SMART Goals

Using the SMART method is an effective way to set clear and realistic financial goals. The word *SMART* is an acronym that helps you create goals that are easier to follow and achieve. Each goal should be specific, measurable, achievable, relevant, and time bound.

Specific: For each goal, you should clearly explain what is being saved or planned for, such as saving money for a new television.

Measurable: You also need a way to measure progress on a goal, usually by setting a dollar amount, such as saving $500.

Achievable: A goal should be realistic based on your income and expenses. A goal that is too large or unrealistic can make it harder to stay motivated.

Relevant: Goals should also be relevant to your needs or plans, such as saving for college, a car, or an emergency fund.

Time bound: Set a clear deadline for the goal, such as saving $500 in six months.

Without clear goals, it can be easy to spend money quickly on small things and end up with nothing left for larger plans.

income, changes may be needed to reduce spending. If income exceeds expenses, the extra money can be used to build savings or pay off debt. Once income and expenses are clearly tracked, it becomes easier to organize spending, set financial goals, and create a realistic budget that works.

Setting Financial Goals

It is important to set goals when making a budget. Goals help you decide what you want to do with your money and why saving matters. Without clear goals, it can be easy to spend money quickly on things and end up with nothing left for larger plans.

Financial goals can be short- or long-term. Short-term goals are things someone wants to achieve soon, usually within a few weeks or months. For teens, short-term goals might include saving money for new clothes, video games, concert tickets, or a school trip. Long-term goals take more time and planning. These might include saving for a car, college, or moving into a first apartment.

When setting financial goals, it helps to make them specific and realistic. A clear goal is easier to reach than a vague one. For example, instead of saying "save more money," a better goal might be "save $800 for a laptop by the end of the summer." This gives a clear amount and a deadline, which helps guide spending choices.

Another helpful strategy is to break big goals into smaller steps. If a teen wants to save $800 and earns $50 per week from a part-time job, setting aside $15 to $20 per week can slowly build toward the goal. Smaller steps make large goals feel more manageable.

Budgets can include different types of goals. Some are savings goals, such as building an emergency fund or saving for something important. Spending goals include planning how much money to allocate to entertainment or hobbies, and giving goals set aside money for donations or helping others. No matter your goal, you can stay motivated to achieve it by writing it down and regularly reviewing its progress.

"Budgeting helps me to not overspend on random things I want. Instead, it lets me make sure I set aside money for my expenses or save for future goals."[13]

—Dallin Gariety, a teen who uses a budget

For Gariety, budgeting helps him make sure he is working toward his financial goals, both short- and long-term ones, while still having some money for fun. "My budgets allow me to save money for college, pay for half of my various expenses, and have money left over to spend on whatever I want." He says, "I get most of my money from working a part-time job as a lifeguard. The rest I usually get from gifts. Budgeting helps me to not overspend on random things I want. Instead, it lets me make sure I set aside money for my expenses or save for future goals."[13]

Creating a Budget

No one budgeting method works for everyone. People choose different budget types based on their money habits, spending needs, and savings goals.

One popular method is the 50/30/20 budget. Using this method, 50 percent of income is spent on needs such as rent or mortgage payments, utilities, insurance, car payments, gas,

Smarter Spending

Many people are guilty of impulse spending from time to time. They buy something on a whim, without planning or careful thought. The decision to impulse spend is often based on emotions, excitement, or a perceived sale rather than an actual need. Impulse spending can quickly derail your financial plans, but you can prevent this by asking a few simple questions before making a purchase. These questions can help you make smarter spending choices:

- Do I truly *need* this? Needs include things like food, housing, and school supplies, whereas wants are items that are nice to have but not essential.
- Can I afford it right now? Spending more than the available budget can lead to financial stress or debt.
- Will I still want this in a week or a month? Waiting before buying something can prevent impulse purchases.
- Is this helping me reach my financial goals? Thinking about savings and plans can help guide better spending decisions and build strong money habits over time.

groceries, and other basic household expenses. Thirty percent of income can be used for discretionary spending or wants, such as gifts, hobbies, vacations, and entertainment. Finally, 20 percent of income goes toward financial goals, such as savings and retirement. For example, if you earn $400 in net pay per month from a part-time job, you will allocate $200 of your net pay to your monthly needs, including car insurance, gas, school supplies, and cell phone bill. You will then have $120 a month, or 30 percent, to spend on wants, such as going to the movies with friends, eating out, and buying the latest video game. Finally, you will put $80, or 20 percent of your net pay, into your savings account, perhaps to help cover future college expenses.

Another strategy is a zero-based budget. With this method, your net pay minus your expenses should equal zero each month. For example, if you earn $2,000 a month, you will allocate every dollar into an expense category, such as rent, groceries, transportation, nonessential spending, savings, and other financial goals.

The pay-yourself-first method emphasizes savings. Using this method, you set a monthly savings goal. With each paycheck, you put that amount into savings to "pay" yourself. Then, you can spend the remaining money however you want, as long as you do not overspend or go into debt.

Needs vs. Wants

One of the most important budgeting skills is understanding the difference between needs and wants. Needs are things required for daily life, whereas wants are things that are enjoyable but not necessary. For teens, examples of needs might include school supplies, basic clothing, transportation to school or work, and lunch money. Examples of wants could include a new video game, concert tickets, streaming subscriptions, or eating out. These items can be fun, but they are not required.

Sometimes, the difference between needs and wants is not so clear. For example, a teen might need a basic cell phone to communicate with friends and family. However, the latest smartphone model might be a want. Similarly, a pair of sneakers is a need for most teens, but a second pair of expensive designer sneakers is a want. Learning to distinguish between needs and wants can help you make smarter spending and budgeting decisions.

Maintain and Review a Budget

A budget should be reviewed regularly to ensure spending and saving remain on track. Looking at a budget each week or month shows whether income and expenses match the plan. "[Budgeting] helps you to stay in control . . . because you really know where every dollar is going, and you can adjust accordingly,"[14] says Jasmine Taylor, founder and chief executive officer (CEO) of Baddies & Budgets, a financial education platform.

> "[Budgeting] helps you to stay in control . . . because you really know where every dollar is going, and you can adjust accordingly."[14]
>
> —Jasmine Taylor, founder and CEO of Baddies & Budgets, a financial education platform

Reviewing a budget can also reveal changes that need to be made. For example, some expenses may be higher than expected, or there may be extra money that can be saved. During the school year, teens might find they need more money for gas. During the summer, they might

A budget should be reviewed regularly to ensure savings and spending remain on track. Looking at a budget each week or month shows whether income and expenses, such as vet bills, match the plan.

be able to work more hours and earn more income. Updating the budget helps keep financial goals realistic and achievable.

Budgets should be flexible. As your life changes, your budget should also change. A new job might change income. Moving into a new apartment will change your rent and living costs. Getting a dog will add new expenses. Using a budget can help you plan for and adjust to life changes.

A Budgeting Success Story

Chris first learned about the importance of budgeting as an adult. He wanted to gain more control over his money and meet his savings goals. "I always thought budgeting was some tedious process of writing stuff down and keeping receipts. But once I learned what it actually meant, it just became so easy,"[15] he says. After going through his income and expenses, Chris set a goal of saving $1,500 a month for a year. He set targets for expense categories and looked for ways to reduce his spending. If he did not spend the full amount that he had budgeted for a specific expense, he moved the extra money into his savings.

Chris explains that using a budgeting app to keep track of his purchases made the process easier. Using a budget to be more aware of where his money is going has also given him more freedom. Now, when an unexpected expense occurs, Chris does not panic. "The other day, the check engine light in my car came on. I had to spend $474, and I didn't even have to go into my emergency fund to cover it," he says. When he finds extra money, Chris moves it into savings. For example, if he budgeted $100 for restaurants but only spent $60 that month, he will move the extra $40 into his savings account. "I make myself not spend that extra money. I move it into my savings that day," Chris says. These deposits may seem small, but over time they can have a big impact on savings. "Little amounts add up,"[16] he says.

Chris believes budgeting can work for everyone. "I think when people think about budgeting, they think about accounting. Like you're just sitting there in an office with no windows. But be open to learning about it—because it actually improves your life," he says. Chris gives another piece of advice to those starting out with budgeting: Be patient. "It's going to take a month or two to get the hang of it. But it can literally change your life. You can quit being stressed about money—and it's very easy."[17]

CHAPTER THREE

Saving, Investing, and Building Wealth

Saving money for the future is one of the best ways to build financial security. There are two main types of savings: short-term and long-term. Short-term savings are funds set aside for emergencies or expenses that may happen soon. This money should be easily accessible when needed. Long-term savings are funds set aside for future financial goals, such as retirement or a major purchase, like a home. In many cases, long-term savings can be invested so the money grows over time.

Why Saving Is Important

Saving money regularly is essential to any financial plan. Through saving, you can protect yourself from unexpected expenses and build wealth for the future. Emergencies happen to everyone. A broken phone, medical expenses, or car repairs can cost hundreds or even thousands of dollars that were not planned for in a monthly budget. Although you cannot predict emergencies, you can be prepared by having money in savings to pay for them. Without savings, you might need to borrow money or use credit cards to pay these unexpected bills, which often leads to debt.

Saving also helps you reach your financial goals. Many financial goals involve large purchases such as buying a car, paying for college, starting a business, or traveling. Saving a little money regularly makes these financial goals possible, especially if placed in accounts that earn interest or investments that increase in value over time.

Emergencies happen to everyone. Fixing a broken-down car can cost hundreds or even thousands of dollars that were not planned for in a monthly budget.

Bank Accounts

One of the simplest and safest ways to save money is to open a savings account at a bank or credit union. They offer a range of accounts to meet different financial needs, such as checking and savings accounts, high-yield savings accounts, and certificates of deposit (CDs).

A checking account holds money for everyday spending. Money can be easily accessed using debit cards, checks, or online payments. A checking account allows you to pay bills, withdraw cash, and make purchases. It usually earns little or no interest, and its main purpose is to offer easy access to money.

A savings account stores money that will not be spent immediately. These accounts earn interest, meaning the bank pays a small amount of interest for keeping money in the account. Savings accounts help you separate money meant for future use from money used for daily spending. Some banks offer high-yield savings accounts that pay higher interest rates than regular savings accounts. Higher interest rates allow savings to grow faster over time.

A CD is a type of savings account that requires money to remain in the account for a set period, such as six months, one year, or several years. Because the money is locked in for the period, CDs offer higher interest rates than regular savings accounts. However, withdrawing money early from a CD may result in a penalty fee.

Pay Yourself First

One of the most effective saving strategies is the pay-yourself-first method. This strategy encourages you to set aside savings immediately upon receiving income, instead of saving whatever money remains after spending. For example, if you earn money from a part-time job or allowance, a portion of that income would be moved into savings right away. The remaining money can then be spent. This method makes saving a priority rather than an afterthought. "When you pay yourself first, you treat saving money as a nonnegotiable expense," says Michelle Troha, the chief marketing officer of First Florida Credit Union. "Before spending a single dollar, you automatically deposit a portion of your paycheck into savings—no excuses."[18]

> **"When you pay yourself first, you treat saving money as a nonnegotiable expense. Before spending a single dollar, you automatically deposit a portion of your paycheck into savings—no excuses."[18]**
>
> —Michelle Troha, chief marketing officer of First Florida Credit Union

Many financial experts suggest saving at least 10 to 20 percent of income when possible. Even smaller amounts can make a difference if saved regularly. Some banks allow automatic transfers from checking accounts to savings accounts, which can make it easier to save consistently. "When you automatically transfer a set amount, it actually simplifies your budgeting as well. For example, if your paycheck is $2,000 and you automatically save $100, you mentally adjust your budget to $1,900, helping you manage expenses without thinking twice,"[19] says Troha.

Jessica Wright has successfully used the pay-yourself-first method to build up savings for her real estate investment business. "When I started, I struggled to save for property down payments

The Rule of 72

The Rule of 72 is a simple way to estimate how long it will take for money to double in value when it earns interest. The rule works by dividing 72 by the annual interest rate. The answer estimates how many years it will take for an investment to double. For example, at a 6 percent annual interest rate, it would take about twelve years (72 ÷ 6 = 12) for the money to double. The Rule of 72 illustrates the power of compound interest. It is frequently used in financial planning to estimate how investments will grow over time or how quickly debt can increase if interest rates are high.

because I waited to see what was left at the end of each month,"[20] she says. Wright then set up automatic transfers that moved 30 percent of her income into a separate savings account each payday. Before long, she had enough savings to buy three investment properties.

Building an Emergency Fund

One of the first priorities when saving is to establish an emergency fund. This is money set aside specifically for unexpected expenses. Cars break down, people get sick, appliances stop working, and jobs can be lost. Without an emergency fund, these situations often lead to borrowing money or using credit cards. An emergency fund helps you pay these bills without creating debt. Yet despite the benefits, less than half of Americans have an adequate emergency savings fund. Nearly one-fourth have no emergency savings at all, according to a 2025 Bankrate survey.

"Worst-case scenario, this is the money that is going to cover your expenses in the event of a loss of income. So, that's why it's important to think of this as three months' worth of expenses or ideally six months' worth of expenses."[21]

—Greg McBride, chief financial analyst at Bankrate

Financial experts often recommend saving enough money in an emergency fund to cover living expenses for three to six months. "Worst-case scenario, this is the money that is going to cover your expenses in the event of a loss of income. So, that's why it's important to think of this as three months' worth of expenses or ideally six months' worth of expenses,"[21] says Greg

McBride, the chief financial analyst at Bankrate. Emergency funds should be kept in safe, easily accessible places, such as a bank or credit union savings account. Account holders can quickly access the money if needed.

After being hit with several large, unplanned expenses, Keri made it a priority to build up her emergency savings fund. "I started by saving only $5 per week, which was all I could afford at the time," she says. "But it felt good even putting aside that small amount, and I soon gained momentum and upped the amount to $10, then $20 per week. Small, regular amounts soon add up."[22]

Compound Interest and How Money Grows

When money is held in a savings account, the bank pays interest on the balance. The bank pays this interest to the account holder for letting the bank use the money while it is stored there. The bank calculates interest as a small percentage, called an interest rate, on the account's balance. Over time, interest adds to the account balance, allowing the savings to grow.

Financial experts often recommend saving enough money in an emergency fund to cover three to six months of living expenses.

"Committing to a specific savings rate and continuing to increase that year after year is what's going to have the biggest impact early in your savings career to get you started."[23]

—Ross Menke, certified financial planner

Many savings accounts also pay compound interest, meaning interest is earned on both the original deposit and the interest already added to the account. Compound interest creates a snowball effect, allowing money to grow faster over time. For example, a savings account holding $1,000 earns 5 percent interest each year. After one year, the interest earned is $50, and the account balance grows to $1,050. In the second year, interest is earned on $1,050 instead of the original $1,000. Interest is $52.50, and the balance grows to $1,102.50. Over time, the account continues to grow. The earlier that saving and investing begin, the more powerful compound interest becomes. "Committing to a specific savings rate and continuing to increase that year after year is what's going to have the biggest impact early in your savings career to get you started,"[23] says Ross Menke, a certified financial planner.

Investing Basics

After you establish an emergency fund, you may want to invest some money. Common types of investments include stocks, bonds, mutual funds, real estate, and retirement accounts. When deciding to invest, you should always consider when you will need that money. For example, you might plan to use it for a vacation (short term), a down payment on a house (medium term), or retirement (long term).

The timeline affects what type of investment to buy. "If you need the money available in a couple years, then it shouldn't be invested in the stock market. It should be invested in those more secure vehicles like a CD or money market where, yes, you might be giving up some potential growth, but it's more important to have the return of your money instead of a return on your money,"[24] says Menke.

Bonds: Lending Money

When someone buys a bond, they are lending money in exchange for regular interest payments. The federal government, state governments, cities, or businesses can issue bonds. The organization that issues the bond promises to pay interest over time and repay the full amount borrowed. The bond's maturity date is the date the loan must be repaid. Bonds are often considered less risky than stocks, but they typically offer lower investment returns.

Investors may hold bonds until maturity or sell them to other investors before then. Bonds can be sold at their face value, also called par value, or at a price above or below that amount. If market interest rates fall below the bond's stated interest rate, the bond becomes more attractive and may sell at a premium, or above its face value. On the other hand, if market interest rates rise above the bond's rate, the bond may sell at a discount, or less than its face value.

Some government bonds offer tax benefits. For example, interest earned from US Treasury bonds and savings bonds is not subject to state or local income taxes. In many cases, interest from municipal bonds, issued by state or local governments, may be free from federal income tax and, in some cases, state taxes as well. Because of these tax advantages, municipal bonds are often popular with investors with higher incomes who want to reduce the taxes they pay on investment earnings.

US Savings Bonds

US savings bonds are issued and backed by the federal government. Because the government guarantees them, investors will never receive less money than they originally invested if the bond is held until maturity. Savings bonds can usually be purchased in amounts ranging from about $50 to $10,000. There are several types of savings bonds. One common type is the Series I bond, which is designed to protect against inflation. The interest rate on a Series I bond combines a fixed rate with a rate that changes based on inflation. This means the bond's earnings can rise when the cost of living increases. People who own paper savings bonds can register them online through TreasuryDirect, a website run by the US Department of the Treasury. Registering bonds online makes them easier to manage and prevents problems if the paper copy is lost.

Stocks: Owning Part of a Company

When someone buys common stock, they are buying a small share of a company. People who own stock are called stockholders or shareholders. Stockholders can earn money in two main ways. The first is through dividends, payments a company makes to its shareholders from its profits. Investors can also make money through stock appreciation, when a stock's price increases over time. If a company performs well, earns strong profits, and grows its business, the value of its stock may rise. Investors can then sell their shares for more than they originally paid. However, investing in stocks always involves risk. If a company does not perform well or loses money, its stock price may fall, and the investor will lose money instead.

Because of this risk, investors should research a company before buying its stock. Investors often look at the company's past financial performance, leadership team, products, and overall business strategy. They may also study how the company's stock price has changed over time or what financial experts say about the company. Investors who take time to learn and stay informed are usually better prepared to make smart investment decisions.

Investments such as stocks, bonds, and mutual funds can be purchased in several ways. Some people work with a full-service broker, who provides advice and helps manage investments.

Mutual Funds: Investing in Many Companies

Instead of buying stock in a single company, investors can buy shares of a mutual fund. A mutual fund usually invests in many companies, buying stocks, bonds, or other investments. By investing in more than one company, the mutual fund diversifies its investments. Diversification helps to reduce risk because an investment does not depend on the success of a single company. If one investment performs poorly, others in the fund may still do well.

Different mutual funds have different levels of risk. Some funds invest mainly in stocks, which can offer higher returns but also greater risk. Others invest mostly in bonds, which are usually more stable but may grow more slowly. Mutual funds are typically managed by investment professionals who make the fund's investment decisions and charge a fee for these services.

Investments such as stocks, bonds, and mutual funds can be purchased in several ways. Some people work with a full-service broker, who provides advice and helps manage investments. Others use a discount broker, which allows investors to buy and sell investments at a lower cost but with less guidance. In some cases, investors can also buy shares directly from certain companies or mutual fund providers.

Risk and Diversification

All investments involve some level of risk. Risk means there is a chance that an investment may lose value. Some investments are riskier than others. Stocks often experience larger price changes, whereas bonds and savings accounts tend to be more stable.

Diversification manages investment risk by spreading money across different types of investments rather than putting it all in one place. For example, instead of buying stock in only one company, an investor might buy a mutual fund that includes hundreds of companies. If one company performs poorly, other investments may perform better, offsetting the loss. Diversification helps reduce the chance that a single bad investment will cause major financial damage.

Building Wealth over Time

Building wealth does not happen overnight. It is the result of consistent habits practiced over many years. People who build wealth often follow several key strategies. They save regularly and do not spend more than their income. They avoid unnecessary debt, set clear financial goals, and invest money for long-term growth.

Even small financial decisions can make a big difference over time. Saving a few dollars each week may not seem significant, but over many years those savings can grow substantially. Learning these habits early in life provides a strong foundation for long-term financial success.

CHAPTER FOUR

Credit, Debt, and Borrowing Responsibly

Sometimes people need to make important purchases—such as buying a house or a car or paying for college—but they do not have enough cash saved. When this occurs, they can borrow money instead. Borrowing allows them to use money now and pay it back later. Borrowing money can be a helpful financial tool when used carefully. However, borrowing money also comes with responsibilities. If debt is not managed carefully, it can lead to stress and long-term financial problems.

Debt as a Financial Tool

Debt is money owed to another person, bank, or company. As a financial tool, debt can help you reach important life goals. It can help you make large purchases that you cannot afford all at once. For example, many people borrow money to buy a home or a car. Without loans, these purchases would be much more difficult.

Borrowing can help teens invest in their future. Student loans, for example, allow young people to pay for college or trade school. Education can lead to better job opportunities and a higher income later in life. Responsible borrowing helps build a strong credit history. A good credit history can make it easier to qualify for future loans and may even lead to lower interest rates.

Matthew Barker is the founding partner of Clarity Wealth, a financial planning firm. He helps clients understand how debt can be a useful tool for achieving their financial goals. "Debt often gets a bad rap, and for good reason—especially when it spirals out of

> "Good debt is the kind that helps increase your net worth or generates long-term income. When managed responsibly, it can be a smart financial tool."[25]
>
> —Matthew Barker, founding partner of Clarity Wealth

control. But not all debt is created equal. In fact, some types of debt can actually help you build long-term wealth when used strategically," Barker says. For example, certain types of debt, such as mortgages, student loans, and business loans, can be beneficial. "Good debt is the kind that helps increase your net worth or generates long-term income. When managed responsibly, it can be a smart financial tool,"[25] he says.

The Cost of Debt

However, debt is not free. When you borrow money, you promise to repay the original loan and also pay the lender interest on the outstanding balance. Interest is the cost of borrowing money and is usually calculated as a percentage of debt. For example, a bank may charge 5 percent interest on a $1,000 loan. If you repay the loan after one year, you will have to pay the bank $1,000 for the original loan and $50 in interest. Interest on debt can grow quickly, especially if the debt is left unpaid for a long time.

Debt can also cause stress. If payments become too large or your income suddenly drops, you may struggle to keep up with bills. Missing payments can damage your credit score and make future borrowing more difficult. Sometimes, people borrow too much money. If they take on more debt than they can afford to repay, it can cause significant financial problems.

Credit Cards and Loans

Two of the most common types of debt are credit cards and loans. Many adults have credit cards. Credit cards allow people to borrow money up to a certain limit. Each time they use a credit card to pay for goods or services, they are borrowing money from the bank or credit card company. At the end of the month, the bank sends a statement listing all charges made with the credit card during that billing period. If they pay the balance in full by the due date, they usually do not have to pay any interest. However, if they do not pay the credit card balance in full each month, the bank will charge interest and add it to the remaining balance owed.

Credit cards often have higher interest rates than other forms of borrowing. In addition, the interest on credit card debt is often compounded daily, meaning it accrues each day on the outstanding balance after the statement due date. The accrued interest increases the outstanding balance daily, and more interest is owed on it. Because of this, carrying a balance on a credit card can quickly become very expensive. "For example, let's say you have a $1,400 balance from multiple dinners out and events with friends on a credit card with a 19.99% APR [annual percentage rate]," says Bola Sokunbi, a certified financial education instructor. "If your minimum payment is $70 a month, it would take you 25 months to pay it off, paying over $300 in interest." [26] As a result, financial experts often recommend paying credit card balances in full each month whenever possible. "I almost always pay it off

Most people borrow money to buy a home. Without loans, such a large purchase would be impossible for many people.

in full at the end,"[27] says Jim Droske, president of Illinois Credit Services, a credit counseling company.

Loans are another common form of credit. With a loan, a lender gives a borrower a specific amount of money that must be repaid over time. Loans usually involve regular monthly payments until the full amount is repaid. Some common types of loans include an auto loan to buy a car, a mortgage to buy a house, a student loan to pay for education, and personal loans, which can be used for many purposes. Loans often have lower interest rates than credit cards, but they still increase the total cost of the purchase.

Credit History and Credit Score

When someone applies for a loan or credit card, lenders want to know whether the borrower is likely to repay the money. To make this decision, lenders consider several factors, including the borrower's credit report, credit score, job history, and income. A credit report contains a record of how the person has handled credit in the past, and this information is used to calculate a credit score. A credit score is a number that predicts how likely the person is to repay borrowed money on time. In general, the higher the credit score, the less risky the borrower appears to the lender.

If a credit report shows late or missed payments, or unpaid accounts, the credit score will usually be lower. A low credit score

Student Loans

Education can be expensive, especially at colleges and universities. Many students use student loans to help pay for tuition, books, housing, and other costs. Student loans typically fall into two main categories: federal student loans and private student loans. The government provides federal student loans, which often have lower interest rates and more flexible repayment options. In comparison, private student loans are offered by banks or other lenders and may have higher interest rates and fewer protections.

Most student loans do not need to be repaid until after students finish school. However, they must eventually be repaid. If students borrow too much, it can take many years to pay off their student loans. For this reason, financial experts often advise students to borrow only what they truly need and to explore scholarships, grants, and other financial aid options before taking on loans.

A credit report contains a record of how someone has handled credit in the past, and this information is used to calculate a credit score.

can make it harder to get approved for loans or credit cards. It can also lead to higher interest rates. "Your score not only can mean the difference between getting or not getting a mortgage or car loan, but also how much it will cost you to borrow that money. And that can translate into paying—or saving—thousands of dollars over time,"[28] says Cindy Scott, a senior manager at investment firm Charles Schwab.

The most important part of a credit score is payment history, which shows whether a person has paid their bills on time. Recent missed payments usually hurt a credit score more than older mistakes. The seriousness of the late payment also matters. For example, a payment that is thirty days late usually affects a credit score less than a payment that is sixty days or more overdue. "Late payments or missing payments can lower your score more than any other factor. Making regular, on-time payments is one of the best ways to bring it back up," says Scott. "That's what I did to improve my own score when I got out of college. And that's what I do today. I also make sure to pay my bills before the due date. Setting up automatic payments makes this pretty painless. Just be sure you have the money in your account to cover them."[29]

Another major factor in a credit score is a person's credit utilization rate. When a credit card company approves a person for a card, they set a limit on how much the person can charge on the card. Similarly, a bank might set a limit on the amount a person can borrow. Credit utilization is the ratio of a person's debt to their total credit limit. Financial experts often suggest keeping debt balances below half of the available credit limit. Lower balances can help show lenders that a borrower is managing credit responsibly.

> **"The more you pay attention to it, the better your credit tends to be."[30]**
>
> —Jim Droske, president of Illinois Credit Services

Improving a credit score takes time. Paying bills on time, keeping credit card balances low, avoiding unnecessary debt, and regularly checking credit reports for errors can help you improve your credit score. "The more you pay attention to it, the better your credit tends to be,"[30] says Droske.

Avoiding Credit Traps

While credit can be useful, it can also lead to financial traps if you borrow too much or do not fully understand the terms of a loan. High-interest debt is one of the biggest dangers. Some loans charge extremely high interest rates, which can cause debt to grow quickly. For example, credit cards and certain short-term loans often have very high fees and interest rates. Borrowers may find themselves trapped in a cycle where they must borrow again just to repay earlier loans.

Another risk is impulse borrowing. Credit cards make it easy to spend money quickly, but purchases made without careful thought can lead to large balances. Advertising and online shopping can also encourage overspending. Many websites offer "buy now, pay later" options that allow shoppers to delay payments. While convenient, these services still create debt that must be repaid.

Amelia's Story

Amelia, an employee of C&N Bank, admits that she learned a hard lesson about credit cards as a young adult. "I signed up for my first credit card shortly after turning 18. I didn't read the fine print or understand how it all worked. To me, it just felt like free money. I used it for everything—clothes, gas, food—and those small splurges added up quickly. I ignored the growing balance until it became overwhelming, and late fees plus high interest only made it worse,"[31] she says.

The impact of Amelia's poor credit decisions hit home when she went to buy a car for the first time. She was declined due to her poor credit. Eventually, she was approved for a car loan, but it had a very high interest rate, making the car purchase more expensive.

The difficulty she had obtaining a car loan was a wake-up call for Amelia. She could no longer ignore her credit card problem. "I cut back on using credit cards and focused on paying more than the minimum balance each month. I also set up reminders to never miss a payment again. Eventually, I paid off my balances. I worked hard to build positive credit by keeping my utilization low and paying on time. I also made a habit of reading the fine print before signing anything," she says. Today, she says that if she could give advice to her younger self about credit cards and debt,

Credit Reporting Agencies

Credit reporting agencies are companies that collect and keep records about how people use credit. The three main agencies in the United States are Equifax, Experian, and TransUnion. These agencies gather information from lenders, such as credit card companies and banks, and create a credit report for individuals. This credit report includes details on payment history, outstanding balances, types of credit, and any late or missed payments. The report also shows a credit score based on the information in it.

Checking a credit report is important because it helps you understand your financial health. It allows you to make sure all the information is correct and up to date. Mistakes or fraud, such as accounts opened without permission, can hurt a credit score. By regularly reviewing reports, you can catch problems early and fix them. A good credit report can make it easier to get loans, rent an apartment, or even get a job.

she would caution that "every swipe adds up and paying the bare minimum isn't enough. Start small and spend only what you can pay off right away to build a strong foundation for the future,"[32] she says.

Managing Debt Wisely

Borrowing money should always involve careful planning. Managing debt wisely means making sure payments are affordable and keeping total debt at a reasonable level. One of the most important strategies to manage debt is creating a budget. A budget helps track income and expenses and shows how much money is available for debt payments. You should try to borrow only what you can comfortably repay within your budget. Making payments on time is also essential. Late payments may result in extra fees and damage your credit score.

Another helpful strategy is to pay more than the minimum payment whenever possible. This can reduce interest costs and help eliminate debt faster. Some people use methods such as the debt

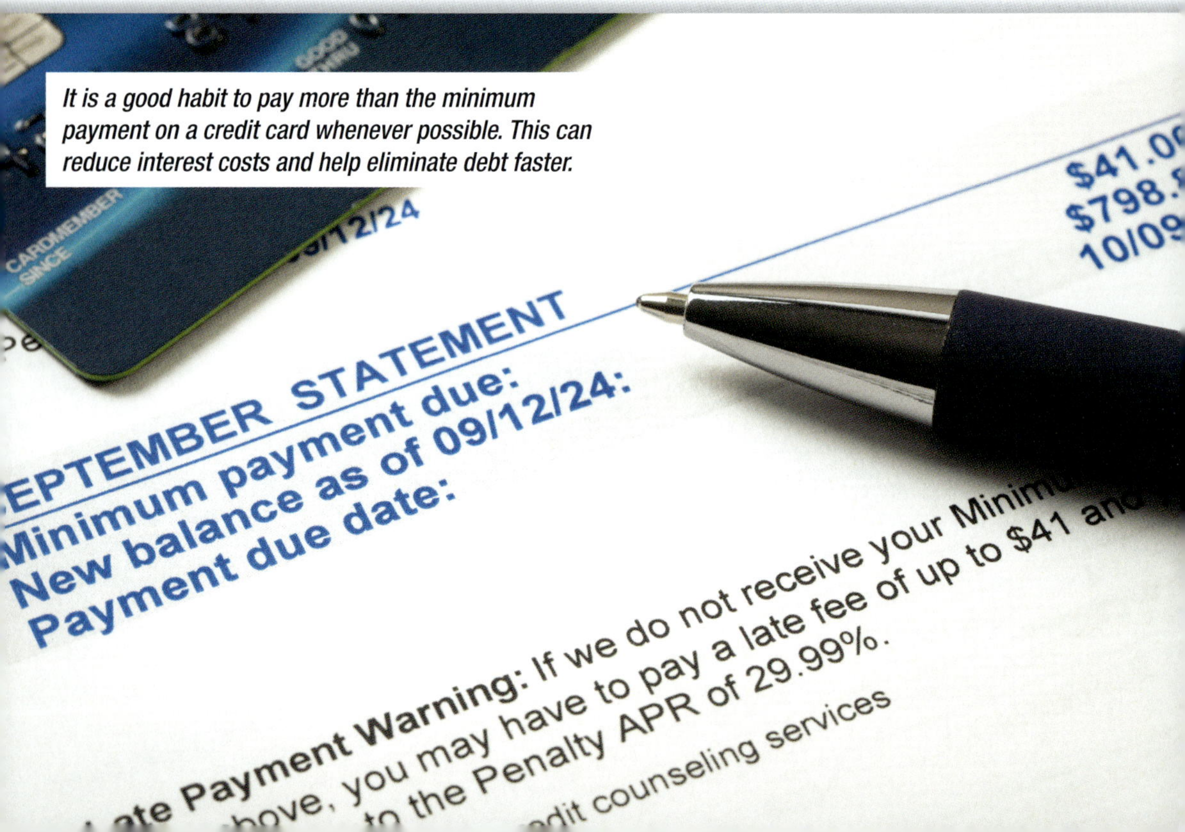

It is a good habit to pay more than the minimum payment on a credit card whenever possible. This can reduce interest costs and help eliminate debt faster.

snowball or debt avalanche strategies to pay off debt. The debt snowball method focuses on paying off smaller debts first, which can create motivation as balances disappear. The debt avalanche method focuses on paying off debts with the highest interest rates first, which can reduce the total interest paid. Both strategies can help people become debt-free over time. "The first step to getting out of debt is total honesty: List every debt, balance, minimum payment, and interest rate," says Trixy Castro, founder of TRX Capital, an investment platform. "You can't fix what you won't face . . . Pick what keeps you consistent. Small shifts—like cutting extras or automating payments—help you take back control."[33]

"Don't be a hostage to your debt. Act now to pay your bills on time, keep debt low, and prove to lenders that you're credit-worthy. Remember, how you use credit today affects what you can do tomorrow."[34]

—Cindy Scott, senior manager at investment firm Charles Schwab

Using Credit Wisely

Credit and borrowing are common parts of modern financial life. When used wisely, they can help you achieve important goals such as education, transportation, or home ownership. However, debt also carries risks. Interest increases the cost of borrowing, and too much debt can cause serious financial problems.

Understanding how credit works, how interest accrues, and how credit scores are calculated helps you make smarter financial decisions. "Building and protecting your credit score takes time and effort, but it's worth it," says Scott. "Don't be a hostage to your debt. Act now to pay your bills on time, keep debt low, and prove to lenders that you're credit-worthy. Remember, how you use credit today affects what you can do tomorrow,"[34] Scott advises. By borrowing carefully, making payments on time, and avoiding unnecessary debt, you can protect your financial future and build strong credit habits that last a lifetime.

CHAPTER FIVE

Protecting and Planning for the Future

Life is full of unexpected events. A person may get sick, lose a job, be in a car accident, or have a home damaged during a storm. Without preparation, these situations can create serious financial problems. A smart financial plan includes steps to protect assets, property, and income while also preparing for long-term goals.

Protecting Assets and Income

A person's assets have value and can help build wealth; assets include bank accounts, investments, homes, cars, and other personal belongings. Income is the money a person earns from working or running a business. Losing either assets or income can put people in a financial hole and make it challenging to pay for everyday needs. For example, when people have medical emergencies, such as a stroke, they incur significant medical bills. And because they cannot work while they are recovering, they often lose income as well. They might have to drain a savings account to pay their bills or run up credit cards to pay for necessities. Before long, they are in financial trouble.

In 2021, sixty-three-year-old Jeff King's doctors performed a surgical procedure called an ablation to normalize his heart rhythm. A few weeks later, King received a hospital bill for $160,000. Because he was uninsured at the time, King was responsible for the entire amount. Eventually, the hospital's financial assistance program reduced the original bill to about

$53,000, but it was still a significant hurdle for King and his wife, Kareen. A few months after the procedure, the Kings sold their home and bought a smaller one. They had planned to use the proceeds from the sale to build their retirement account, but now that money is helping pay the medical debt. King and his wife took part-time jobs to earn extra income and pay down the debt.

To protect assets and manage financial risk, many people buy insurance. Insurance is a financial agreement that helps protect people from large financial losses. When someone buys insurance, they pay an amount of money called a premium to an insurance company. In return, the insurance company helps cover certain costs if a specific event happens. Common types of insurance include health, homeowners' or renters', auto, and life insurance.

Insurance works by spreading financial risk among many people. Everyone pays small premiums, and the insurance company uses that money to help those who experience losses. For example, most people will not have a serious car accident each year. If someone does, the costs can be extremely high. Insurance helps cover those expenses so that one accident does not cause financial disaster. "Here's the truth: a strong financial plan doesn't just build wealth, it protects it," says Domenica Lurvey, a certified financial planner. "The right insurance coverage can act as a stabilizer when life doesn't go according to plan."[35]

"Here's the truth: a strong financial plan doesn't just build wealth, it protects it. The right insurance coverage can act as a stabilizer when life doesn't go according to plan."[35]

—Domenica Lurvey, certified financial planner

Insuring Health, Homes, and Vehicles

Insurance helps guard against financial loss when the unexpected strikes. Health care can be extremely expensive. Doctor visits, medications, surgeries, and hospital stays often cost thousands of dollars. Without adequate health insurance, a single medical emergency could lead to enormous bills. Health insurance helps pay for many of these medical expenses. People with health insurance typically pay monthly premiums. They may also pay smaller amounts when receiving care, such as copayments or deductibles. In return, the insurance company helps cover most medical costs. Many employers offer health insurance as part of employee benefits. Government programs also help some people receive coverage.

A home is one of the most valuable assets many people own. Homeowners' insurance protects houses and personal belongings from damage or loss. It can help cover costs if a home is damaged by fire, storms, theft, and vandalism. The policy may also help pay for temporary housing if a home becomes unlivable after damage. People who rent homes or apartments can also protect their belongings with renters' insurance. It usually costs less than homeowners insurance but still protects against theft, fire, or other damage.

In a car accident, costs can add up quickly. Repairs to damaged vehicles, medical bills, property damage, and even legal fees can add up to tens of thousands of dollars. Auto insurance

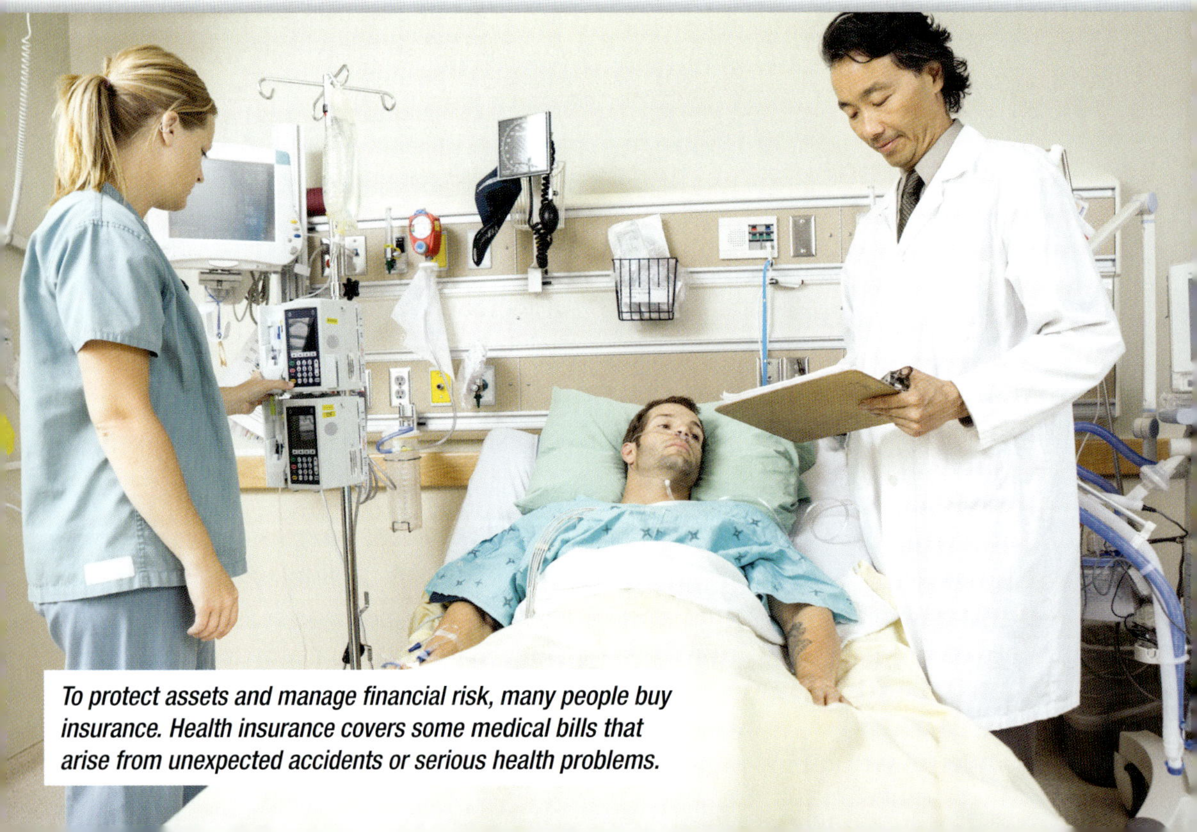

To protect assets and manage financial risk, many people buy insurance. Health insurance covers some medical bills that arise from unexpected accidents or serious health problems.

protects drivers in the event of a car accident. In most states, drivers are required by law to carry at least basic auto insurance. Different policies provide different levels of protection. Some policies cover only damage to others, whereas more comprehensive policies cover damage to the driver's own car as well.

Life Insurance

When a person dies, family members must deal with the financial consequences. If that person was a household's primary earner, the sudden loss of income can cause significant disruption. Without that income, a family may struggle to pay household bills, make mortgage payments, and save for education expenses. Life insurance helps protect a family financially if a primary earner dies. In the event of a death, the insurance company pays the policy's beneficiaries, usually family members.

> **"Her life insurance policy benefits helped ease the family's worries and provided a layer of financial stability."[36]**
>
> —Erin Janke, friend to a woman who died unexpectedly

Erin Janke's good friend, Krystal, died unexpectedly during the birth of her second child after a rare complication, devastating her family and friends. However, a life insurance policy that thirty-nine-year-old Kristal had purchased two years earlier helped her family during the difficult time. "Her life insurance policy benefits helped ease the family's worries and provided a layer of financial stability," Janke explains. The life insurance benefits, along with coverage from a disability insurance policy, "allowed [Kristal's husband] to take time off from work to grieve, care for their children, and pick up the pieces of his life,"[36] says Janke.

Digital Security

People use computers and smartphones to conduct a wide range of financial activities, including paying bills, shopping, banking, and investing. While these tools make life more convenient, they also create new risks. Cybercriminals use technology to steal

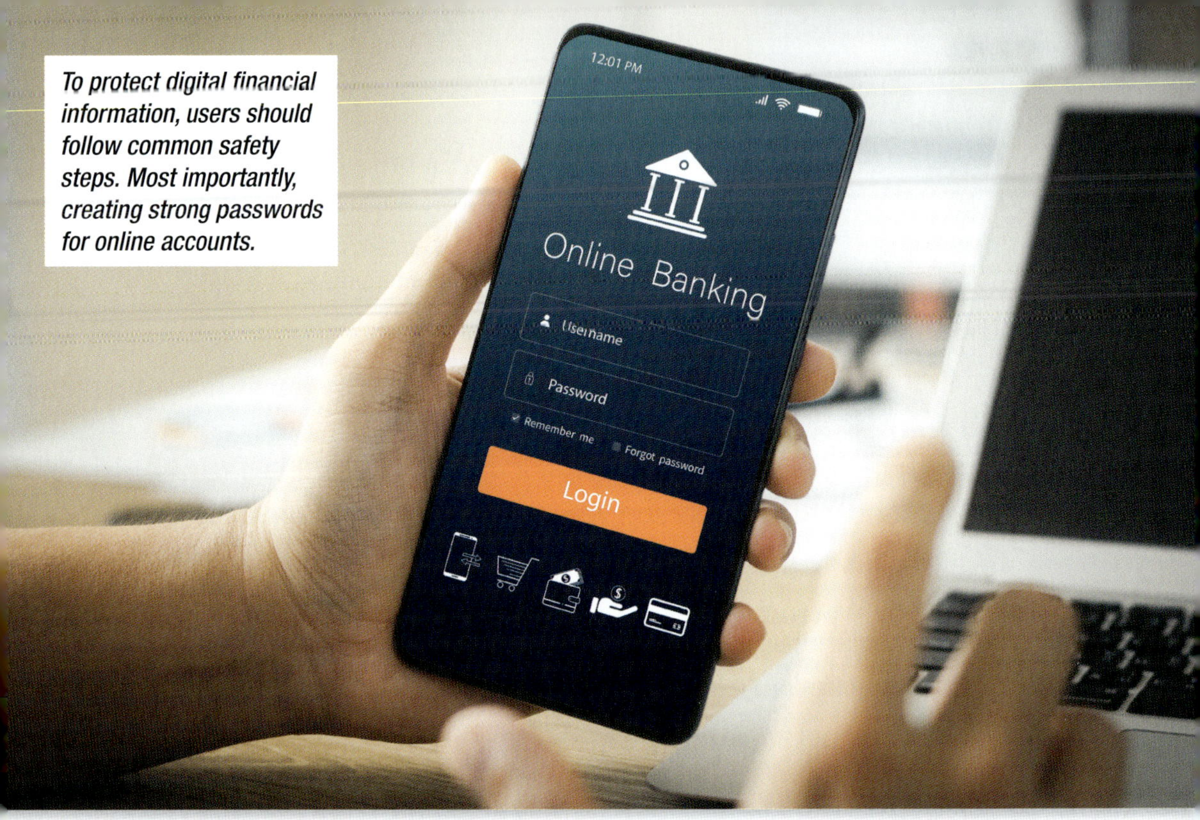

To protect digital financial information, users should follow common safety steps. Most importantly, creating strong passwords for online accounts.

money or personal information. Fraud and scams can take many forms, including fake emails, phone calls, and websites that try to trick people into sharing sensitive information. For these reasons, protecting digital financial information is an important part of financial security.

To protect your digital financial information, you should follow common safety steps. These include creating strong passwords for online accounts and not sharing personal information via email or text messages. Make sure that the websites where you shop and bank online are secure, and regularly update the security software on your computers. In addition, regularly monitor your bank and credit card accounts to quickly spot unusual activity.

Retirement Planning Basics

Part of financial literacy is planning for the future, and one of the biggest financial goals is saving for retirement. Many people will spend twenty to thirty years in retirement, so planning ahead is extremely important. Special retirement savings accounts that offer tax advantages, such as 401(k) plans and individual retirement accounts (IRAs), can help people save for retirement.

Many employers offer 401(k) plans as employee benefits. Employees contribute a portion of their paychecks to their 401(k) accounts. Some employers match part of their employees' contributions and add these additional funds to their accounts. In contrast, IRAs are accounts individuals can use to save for retirement outside of an employer program. Money placed in retirement accounts is typically invested in stocks, bonds, or mutual funds and grows over time.

Starting Early Matters

One of the most powerful tools in long-term financial planning is time. Money saved and invested early has more time to grow. With the power of compound interest, it earns money on the contributions and the interest that has already been earned.

For example, suppose two people save and invest $200 a month and earn an average annual return of 7 percent. The first person begins saving at age twenty-two, but the second person does not start until age thirty-two. By age sixty-five, the first person has saved for forty-three years and has approximately $613,000. The second person has saved for thirty-three years and has about

Identity Theft Protection

Identity theft occurs when someone steals another person's personal information and uses it for financial gain. Criminals may steal social security numbers, birth dates, and bank account numbers to open credit accounts, make purchases, or apply for loans in someone else's name. Identity theft can cause serious financial problems and damage credit scores. A lower credit score can make it harder to get a loan, rent an apartment, or qualify for lower interest rates.

To protect against identity theft, be careful to keep personal information secure and do not share your social security number or other sensitive data. Regularly review your credit report to spot any unauthorized activity early. In addition, you can use identity theft monitoring services that alert you to unusual activity on your credit report and help you resolve any fraud.

$294,000. Even though there is only a ten-year difference, the first person's account is more than twice the second person's. This example illustrates why starting early, even with small amounts, can have a big impact on long-term financial goals.

> "I wanted to start saving early because the more the money sits, the more it compounds, the more it's going to grow."[37]
>
> —Brynnley Beckman, biology teacher

Brynnley Beckman teaches ninth-grade biology at the Shelton School in Dallas. Although she is only twenty-three, she is already saving for retirement. Beckman contributes 3 percent of each paycheck to an employer-sponsored retirement account. "I wanted to start saving early because the more the money sits, the more it compounds, the more it's going to grow," she says. Beckman is saving now to be financially independent later in life: "I could retire at the age that I want to, rather than working later, and have financial freedom and security."[37]

The Impact of Inflation

Money saved today is not worth the same in the future. This occurs because of inflation, the increase in the prices of goods and services over time. When prices rise, each dollar buys fewer things than it did before. For example, a gallon of milk might cost three dollars today. If inflation continues, that same gallon of milk might cost four dollars or more several years later. Because of inflation, money saved today may lose some of its purchasing power in the future. "Inflation quietly erodes purchasing power over time," says Lurvey. "The same

Disability Insurance

Losing the ability to work can happen unexpectedly to anyone. Without a steady income, it can be difficult to cover basic living costs. In such cases, disability insurance can protect income for people who are unable to work because of illnesses or injuries. Instead of covering medical bills, it replaces part of their paycheck so they can still pay for everyday expenses such as rent, food, and bills. Short-term disability insurance only covers people for a few weeks or months, but long-term disability insurance can last for years or even until retirement. Disability insurance provides financial security during a difficult time. It helps to protect people's financial futures and prevent debt, enabling them to focus on recovery instead of worrying about money.

Money saved today is not worth the same in the future. This is because prices rise over time, a concept known as inflation, and each dollar buys fewer things than it did before.

dollar that comfortably covered expenses ten years ago may not stretch as far today. For retirees living on fixed or semi-fixed income, this slow change can meaningfully affect how long savings last."[38]

Inflation affects many parts of daily life, including groceries, housing costs, transportation, health care, and education. Because of inflation, simply saving money in cash may not be enough to maintain its value over time. Investing money can help it grow faster than inflation. Investments such as stocks, bonds, and mutual funds have historically provided higher long-term returns than savings accounts alone.

As a certified financial planner, Lurvey works with clients to develop strong retirement financial plans. She factors inflation into each plan and helps her clients understand how it may affect their goals. "While inflation is unpredictable, your plan doesn't have to be," she says. One of Lurvey's clients wanted to understand how higher prices due to inflation might force them to retire later than they had initially planned. "By modeling several inflation scenarios, we found that small spending adjustments could keep their plan on track,"[39] Lurvey explains.

Building a Strong Financial Future

Protecting money and planning ahead are essential to a strong financial plan. Insurance protects you from large financial losses caused by accidents, illness, or disasters. "Insurance isn't about fearing the worst," says Lurvey. "It's about making sure that even if the unexpected happens, your goals and values stay intact."[40] Digital security and identity protection help prevent fraud and theft. At the same time, long-term planning helps you prepare for major life events, such as retirement. Saving early and investing wisely can help your money grow over time.

Financial security does not happen overnight. It develops through consistent habits, careful planning, and responsible decision-making. "Hope is not a strategy, and luck is not a reliable plan," says Daniel Pick, an estate planning partner with the law firm Davis Miles in Arizona. "The best way to secure the future you want is through careful planning, informed decision-making, and proactive steps toward your goals."[41] By learning how to protect assets and plan for the future, you can build a stronger financial foundation.

SOURCE NOTES

Introduction: The Basics of Financial Health

1. Quoted in Dave Cruz, "Students Get Crash Course in Financial Literacy," *Rocky Mount Telegram,* January 17, 2026. www.rockymounttelegram.com.
2. Quoted in Cruz, "Students Get Crash Course in Financial Literacy."
3. Quoted in Cruz, "Students Get Crash Course in Financial Literacy."
4. Quoted in Queensborough National Bank & Trust Company, "Financial Literacy Is Vital—Henry's Success Story." www.qnbtrust.bank.

Chapter One: Money and Income

5. Quoted in TransUnion, "More Than One-Third of Gig Workers Rely on Gig Work as Primary Source of Income," October 15, 2024. https://newsroom.transunion.com.
6. Quoted in James Royal, "25 Passive Income Ideas to Help You Make More Money," Bankrate, November 26, 2025. www.bankrate.com.
7. Quoted in Royal, "25 Passive Income Ideas to Help You Make More Money."
8. Quoted in Meakem Group, "Educate and Celebrate Your Teen's First Paycheck," February 3, 2023. https://themeakemgroup.com.
9. Quoted in Krysten Crawford, "Dollars and Sense: The Case for Teaching Personal Finance," Stanford Institute for Economic Policy Research, November 28, 2023. https://siepr.stanford.edu.

Chapter Two: Budgeting and Smart Spending

10. Quoted in Jordan Rosenfeld, "Experts Explain: Why Budgeting Is Key to Growing Your Wealth in 2024 and Where to Start," Yahoo Finance, December 23, 2023. https://finance.yahoo.com.
11. Quoted in Rosenfeld, "Experts Explain."

12. Dallin Gariety, "Teen Article: The Benefits of Budgeting," Sunward. https://gosunward.org.
13. Gariety, "Teen Article."
14. Quoted in Ryan Ermey, "How a 31-Year-Old Built a 'Cash Stuffing' Business on Track to Bring in $1 Million This Year: 'Make Sure You Have the Backbone for It,'" CNBC Make It, May 10, 2023. www.cnbc.com.
15. Quoted in Ramsey Solutions, "How Budgeting Is Helping One Man Save $40,000 This Year," May 1, 2023. www.ramseysolutions.com.
16. Quoted in Ramsey Solutions, "How Budgeting Is Helping One Man Save $40,000 This Year."
17. Quoted in Ramsey Solutions, "How Budgeting Is Helping One Man Save $40,000 This Year."

Chapter Three: Saving, Investing, and Building Wealth

18. Quoted in Cindy Lamothe, "How the 'Pay Yourself First' Budgeting Method Can Help You Stick to Your 2025 Goals," Yahoo Finance, February 12, 2025. https://finance.yahoo.com.
19. Quoted in Lamothe, "How the 'Pay Yourself First' Budgeting Method Can Help You Stick to Your 2025 Goals."
20. Quoted in Lamothe, "How the 'Pay Yourself First' Budgeting Method Can Help You Stick to Your 2025 Goals."
21. Quoted in Rachel DePompa, "Nearly 1 in 4 Americans Have No Emergency Savings, Survey Finds," WHSV, August 21, 2025. www.whsv.com.
22. Quoted in Philippa Prentice, "Real-Life Read: Emergency Savings—How I Got Started," *Real-Life Read Blog,* Sorted, July 25, 2025. https://sorted.org.nz.
23. Quoted in Brian Baker, "How to Invest in Your 20s: 7 Tips to Get Started," Bankrate, February 4, 2025. www.bankrate.com.
24. Quoted in Baker, "How to Invest in Your 20s."

Chapter Four: Credit, Debt, and Borrowing Responsibly

25. Matthew Barker, "Not All Debt Is Bad: How to Use Debt as a Tool—Not a Trap," Clarity Wealth, April 2, 2025. www.claritywealthplan.com.

26. Quoted in Elizabeth Gravier, "In a Year of Asking Experts Credit Card Advice, These Are the 5 Things They Agree On," CNBC Select, December 18, 2025. www.cnbc.com.
27. Quoted in Gravier, "In a Year of Asking Experts Credit Card Advice, These Are the 5 Things They Agree On."
28. Cindy Scott, "How to Improve Your Credit Score in 7 Steps," Charles Schwab, June 11, 2024. www.schwab.com.
29. Scott, "How to Improve Your Credit Score in 7 Steps."
30. Quoted in Gravier, "In a Year of Asking Experts Credit Card Advice, These Are the 5 Things They Agree On."
31. Quoted in C&N Bank, "Credit Confessions: True Stories of Debt, Regret and Second Chances," September 16, 2025. www.cnbankpa.com.
32. Quoted in C&N Bank, "Credit Confessions."
33. Quoted in *Forbes,* "18 Expert-Backed First Steps to Start Reducing Your Debt," August 13, 2025. www.forbes.com.
34. Scott, "How to Improve Your Credit Score in 7 Steps."

Chapter Five: Protecting and Planning for the Future

35. Domenica Lurvey, "How Insurance Strengthens Your Financial Plan," Sachetta, August 6, 2025. https://sachetta.com.
36. Erin Janke, "Real Stories: A Life Insurance Story That Changed Everything," Farmers Insurance, November 3, 2025. www.farmers.com.
37. Quoted in Lisa Rabasca Roepe, "Gen Z, It Turns Out, Is Great at Saving for Retirement," *New York Times*, June 28, 2025. www.nytimes.com.
38. Domenica Lurvey, "The Impact of Inflation on Retirement Planning," Sachetta, December 3, 2025. https://sachetta.com.
39. Lurvey, "The Impact of Inflation on Retirement Planning."
40. Lurvey, "How Insurance Strengthens Your Financial Plan."
41. Daniel Pick, "Don't Rely on Luck: Your Future Is Too Important Not to Plan," Davis Miles, March 18, 2025. www.davismiles.com.

FOR FURTHER RESEARCH

Books

Berna Anat, *Money Out Loud: All the Financial Stuff No One Taught Us*. Quill Tree, 2023.

Ferne Bowe, *Money Skills for Teens: A Beginner's Guide to Budgeting, Saving, and Investing: Everything a Teenager Should Know About Personal Finance*. Bemberton, 2023.

Emily Carter, *Money Skills for Teens: These Are the Things About Money Management and Personal Finance You Must Know but They Didn't Teach You in School*. Skillset Symphony, 2023.

Stephen Krensky, *Money and Finance Field Guide: A How-to Book on Earning, Saving, and Spending Money*. Penguin Young Readers, 2025.

Athena Valentine Lent and Mykail James, *Personal Finance for Teens*. John Wiley & Sons, 2025.

Ruth Owen, *Budgeting*. Bearport, 2023.

Joshua Rivedal, *The Essential Guide to Personal Finance for Teens and College Students: Practical Hacks to Eliminate Money-Stress and Build Wealth for the Future*. Skookum Hill, 2023.

Internet Sources

Brian Baker, "How to Start Investing in Your 20s: 7 Tips to Get Started," Bankrate, February 4, 2025. www.bankrate.com.

John Csiszar, "9 Experts Share Money Advice They Would Give Their Younger Selves." AOL, March 8, 2026. www.aol.com.

LendingClub, "Why Is Budgeting So Important for Financial Success?," April 10, 2025. www.lendingclub.com.

Lisa Rabasca Roepe, "Gen Z, It Turns Out, Is Great at Saving for Retirement," *New York Times*, June 28, 2025. www.nytimes.com.

Websites

American Bankers Association: Youth & Money

www.aba.com/advocacy/community-programs/consumer-resources/kids-money

The American Bankers Association's Youth & Money website provides free resources, lessons, and activities to help children and teens learn important money skills, such as saving, budgeting, and spending wisely. It also offers tips for parents and educators to teach financial responsibility and build strong financial habits from a young age.

Building Wealth

www.dallasfed.org/-/media/microsites/cd/wealth/online/index.html

This financial education resource from the Federal Reserve Bank of Dallas provides basic guidance to individuals and families who wish to develop a plan for building personal wealth.

Consumer Financial Protection Bureau

www.consumerfinance.gov

The Consumer Financial Protection Bureau is a federal agency that ensures consumers are treated fairly by banks and other financial institutions. Its website has a consumer education section with several topics that include loans, credit cards, and fraud.

Experian

www.experian.com

Experian is one of the three main US credit bureaus. Its website has information about credit reports, credit scores, and other related topics.

Federal Student Aid

https://studentaid.gov

Federal Student Aid, a part of the US Department of Education, is the largest provider of student financial aid in the nation. Its website has a link to the Free Application for Federal Student Aid form and information about student aid and loans.

IdentityTheft.gov
www.identitytheft.gov
IdentityTheft.gov is the federal government's one-stop resource for identity theft victims. The site provides information, checklists, and other resources to help identity theft victims.

Schwab Moneywise
www.schwabmoneywise.com
Charles Schwab's Moneywise website is a free educational resource that helps people learn about budgeting, saving, investing, and managing debt. It offers articles, videos, tools, and courses designed to build financial knowledge and support smarter money decisions at any age.

Youth Finance USA
www.youthfinanceusa.org
Youth Finance USA is a nonprofit organization dedicated to teaching kids and teens how to manage money and make smart financial decisions. Its website offers programs, partnerships, and educational resources designed to make financial literacy accessible and engaging for young people across the country.

INDEX

PICTURE CREDITS

Cover: Anna Bergbauer/iStock

5: Drazen Zigic/Shutterstock
9: WBMUL/Shutterstock
10: JarTee/Shutterstock
13: Luis Fernando Davila/Shutterstock
17: MarioGuti/iStock
19: Monkey Business Images/Shutterstock
23: SeventyFour/iStock
26: Master1305/Shutterstock
29: Vitalii Vodolazskyi/Shutterstock
32: Monkey Business Images/Shutterstock
37: Monkey Business Images/Shutterstock
39: Andrew Angelov/Shutterstock
42: Kenishirotie/Shutterstock
46: Tyler Olson/Shutterstock
48: Thapana Onphalai/iStock
51: Sergei Chuyko/Shutterstock

ABOUT THE AUTHOR

Carla Mooney is the author of many books for young adults and children. She lives in Pittsburgh, Pennsylvania, with her husband and three children.